Unle ash C reat ivity

inspiring photography quotes

Marcel Borgstijn

Unleash
Creativity

inspiring
photography quotes

Marcel Borgstijn

ABOUT THE BOOK

This book came forth from my blog www.unleash-creativity.com where I write posts with inspiring photos to unleash your own creativity on photography. I had gathered lots of quotes on creativity and photography and posted them regularly . The collection grew faster than my posts so the idea for this book was born.

I hope you enjoy these quotes.

This book is not supposed to be read from beginning to end but should be opened on a random page.

As I always say on my blog:
Don't copy. Get inspired and get started!

'Beauty can be seen in all things, seeing and composing the beauty is what separates the snapshot from the photograph.' - Matt Hardy

'Photographers mistake the emotion they feel while taking the photo as a judgment that the photograph is good' - Garry Winogrand

'When people ask what equipment I use - I tell them my eyes.' - Anonymous

'I began to realise that film sees the world differently than the human eye, and that sometimes those differences can make a photograph more powerful than what you actually observed.' - Galen Rowell

'I use photography as a way to help me understand why I am here. The camera helps me to see.' - Trent Parke

'My dream concept is that I have a camera and I am trying to photograph what is essentially invisible. And every once in a while I get a glimpse of her and I grab that picture.' – Leonard Nimoy

'Photographers are violent people. First they frame you, then they shoot you, then they hang you on the wall.' – Anonymous

'The world now contains more photographs than bricks, and they are, astonishingly, all different.' – John Szarkowski

'You don't take photos with your camera, you take them with your brain.' – Bambi Cantrell

'All photographs are accurate. None of them is the truth.' – Richard Avedon

'Every time someone tells me how sharp my photos are, I assume that it isn't a very interesting photograph. If it were, they would have more to say.' —
Anonymous

'It is not altogether wrong to say that there is no such thing as a bad photograph – only less interesting, less relevant, less mysterious ones.' – Susan Sontag

'One photo out of focus is a mistake, ten photos out of focus are an experimentation, one hundred photo out of focus are a style.' – Anonymous

'The essential part of creativity is not being afraid to fail.' — Edwin H. Land

'When I say I want to photograph someone, what it really means is that I'd like to know them. Anyone I know I photograph.' — Annie Leibovitz

'A good photograph is the result of making a series of good decisions.' — William Greiner

'Dodging and burning are steps to take care of mistakes God made in establishing tonal relationships.' - Ansel Adams

'I photograph the things that I do not wish to paint, the things which already have an existence.' - Man Ray

'If you want to be a better photographer, stand in front of more interesting stuff.' – Jim Richardson

'Nothing happens when you sit at home. I always make it a point to carry a camera with me at all times... I just shoot at what interests me at that moment.' – Elliott Erwitt

'Photography is nothing – it's life that interests me.' – Henri Cartier-Bresson

'Vision is the art of seeing what is invisible to others.' – Jonathan Swift

'A good photograph is knowing where to stand.' – Ansel Adams

'Creativity is allowing yourself to make mistakes. Art is knowing which ones to keep.' – Scott Adams

'I look at life outside of the lens and capture the world through it.' – Thomas Robinson

'I wish more people felt that photography was an adventure the same as life itself and felt that their individual feelings were worth expressing. To me, that makes photography more exciting.' – Harry Callahan

'Never have I found the limits of the photographic potential. Every horizon, upon being reached, reveals another beckoning in the distance. Always, I am on the threshold.' — W. Eugene Smith

'Photography is a way of feeling, of touching, of loving. What you have caught on film is captured forever... it remembers little things, long after you have forgotten everything.' — Aaron Siskind

'There is a creative fraction of a second when you are taking a picture. Your eye must see a composition or an expression that life itself offers you, and you must know with intuition when to click the camera. That is the moment the photographer is creative. Oop! The Moment! Once you miss it, it is gone forever.' – Henri Cartier-Bresson

'It is more important to click with people than to click the shutter.' - Alfred Eisenstaedt

'There are plenty of beautiful girls who don't photograph well.' - Lauren Hutton

'It is a peculiar part of the good photographer's adventure to know where luck is most likely to lie in the stream, to hook it, and to bring it in without unfair play and without too much subduing it.' – James Agee

'The whole act of creating a photograph is an act of cropping reality.' – Errol Morris

'If I think too much, I don't want to shoot; if I enjoy shooting, I don't want to think.'
– Wei Na

'Once photography enters your bloodstream, it's like a disease, it's infectious.'
– Anonymous

'While photographs may not lie, liars may photograph.' –
Lewis Hine

'I always thought good photos were like good jokes. If you have to explain it, it just isn't that good.' – Anonymous

'No place is boring, if you've had a good night's sleep and have a pocket full of unexposed film.' – Robert Adams

'Unless you photograph what you love, you're not going to make good art.' – Sally Mann

'I love to take photos because people don't have to speak any particular language to understand what I want to say.' – Michael Fanta

'Photography, as we all know, is not real at all. It is an illusion of reality with which we create our own private world.' – Arnold Newman

'Which of my photographs is my favorite? The one I'm going to take tomorrow.' — Imogen Cunningham

'Fear is a darkroom where negatives develop.' — Usman B. Asif

'Photography is a small voice, at best, but sometimes one photograph, or a group of them, can lure our sense of awareness.' — W. Eugene Smith

'To me, photography is an art of observation. It's about finding something interesting in an ordinary place... I've found it has little to do with the things you see and everything to do with the way you see them.' - Elliott Erwitt

'No matter what camera you use, it is not the camera but your artistic eyes which makes the photograph.' - Taga Creekside

'There are no rules for good photographs, there are only good photographs.' — Ansel Adams

'If I saw something in my viewfinder that looked familiar to me, I would do something to shake it up.' — Garry Winogrand

'The viewer must bring their own view to a photograph.' – Fay Godwin

'I never have taken a picture I've intended. They're always better or worse.' – Diane Arbus

'Photography deals exquisitely with appearances, but nothing is what it appears to be.' – Duane Michals

'Everyone has a photographic memory, but not everyone has film.' – Anonymous

'Often something disturbs us more in photographed form than it does when we actually experience it.' – Susan Sontag

'All the technique in the world doesn't compensate for the inability to notice.' - Elliott Erwitt

'It is one thing to photograph people. It is another to make others care about them by revealing the core of their humanness.' - Paul Strand

'Wherever there is light, one can photograph.' - Alfred Stieglitz

'A true photograph
need not be explained,
nor can it be contained
in words.' – Ansel Adams

'In my mind's eye, I visualize how a particular... sight and feeling will appear on a print. If it excites me, there is a good chance it will make a good photograph. It is an intuitive sense, an ability that comes from a lot of practice.' – Ansel Adams

'There will be times when you will be in the field without a camera. And, you will see the most glorious sunset or the most beautiful scene that you have ever witnessed. Don't be bitter because you can't record it. Sit down, drink it in, and enjoy it for what it is!' − DeGriff

'I learned from looking at his (Ansel Adams) work the places he loved the most, and where he spent the most time, was where he did his best work. I learned from him that you have to love what you photograph, and you have to give it time.' − Ion Zupce

'The photograph itself is a greater inspiration rather than the (name of the) photographer.' — Gunnar Smoliansky

'A photograph is usually looked at — seldom looked into.' — Ansel Adams

'Photography can only represent the present. Once photographed, the subject becomes part of the past.' — Berenice Abbott

'Buying a Nikon doesn't make you a photographer. It makes you a Nikon owner.' - Anonymous

'No matter how sophisticated the camera, the photographer is still the one that makes the picture.' - Doug Bartlow

'You can't buy
happiness, but
you can
photograph
people and
that's kind of
the same
thing.' –
Anonymous

'If I could tell the story in words, I wouldn't need to lug around a camera.' – Lewis Hine

'When you photograph people in colour you photograph their clothes. But when you photograph people in B&W, you photograph their souls!' – Ted Grant

'All photos are lies but some are better lies than other.' – Charlie Kirk

'Actually, I'm not all that interested in the subject of photography. Once the picture is in the box, I'm not all that interested in what happens next. Hunters, after all, aren't cooks.' – Henri Cartier-Bresson

'When the shutter closes, the world opens.' – Sharon Wax

'One should really use the camera as though tomorrow you'd be stricken blind.' – Dorothea Lange

'I think a photography class should be a requirement in all educational programs because it makes you see the world rather than just look at it.' – Anonymous

'Landscape photography is the supreme test of the photographer – and often the supreme disappointment.' – Anonymous

'Equipment is merely an instrument to get what he already created in his head.' – Ivo Pervan

'There are always two people in every picture: the photographer and the viewer.' – Ansel Adams

'Photographs are like wine, they get better with age.' – John E. Burkowski

'If your photos aren't good enough, then you're not close enough.' – Robert Capa

'Photographers mistake the emotion they feel while taking the photo as a judgment that the photograph is good' – Garry Winogrand

'When people ask what equipment I use - I tell them my eyes.' – Anonymous

'I hate cameras. They are so much more sure than I am about everything.' – John Steinbeck

'Be yourself. I
much   prefer
seeing
something,
even   it   is
clumsy,   that
doesn't   look
like   somebody
else's   work.' –
William Klein

'Photographs not only show stories but also shape them.' - Benjamin Cawthra

'A photograph is a secret about a secret. The more it tells you the less you know.' - Diane Arbus

'Photograph: a picture painted by the sun without instruction in art.' - Ambroce Bierce

'There is only you and your camera. The limitations in your photography are in yourself, for what we see is what we are.' – Ernst Haas

'A lot of people have taste, but they're not daring enough to be creative.' – Bill Cunningham

'Effective creatives are intrigued by the speed bumps, and not falsely lured by the thrill of acceleration.' – Ric Grefe

'The creative act lasts but a brief moment, a lightning instant of give- and-take, just long enough for you to level the camera and to trap the fleeting prey in your little box.' – Henri Cartier-Bresson

'Creativity exists in the spaces between ideas.' – David Wescott

'Photography is more than a medium for factual communication of ideas. It is a creative art.' – Ansel Adams

'A good snapshot stops a moment from running away.' – Eudora Welty

'Seeing is not enough; you have to feel what you photograph.' – Andre Kertesz

'When you find yourself beginning to feel a bond between yourself and the people you photograph, when you laugh and cry with their laughter and tears, you will know you are on the right track.' – Arthur Fellig

'No man has the right to dictate what other men should perceive, create or produce, but all should be encouraged to reveal themselves, their perceptions and emotions, and to build confidence in the creative spirit.' – Ansel Adams

'When I photograph, what I'm really doing is seeking answers to things.' – Wynn Bullock

'I love the people I photograph. I mean, they're my friends. I've never met most of them or I don't know them at all, yet through my images I live with them.' - Bruce Gilden

'There is no such thing as bad light, only bad photographers.' - J Alan Paul

'Character, like a photograph, develops in darkness.' – Yousuf Karsh

'The goal is not to change your subjects, but for the subject to change the photographer.' – Anonymous

'You cannot depend on your eyes if your imagination is out of focus.'
— Mark Twain

'No place is boring, if you've had a good night's sleep and have a pocket full of unexposed film.' - Robert Adams

You've got to push yourself harder. You've got to start looking for pictures nobody else could take. You've got to take the tools you have and probe deeper. - William Albert Allard

'Art is our defense
against hysteria
and death.' -
Theodore Roethke

'My photographs are not planned or composed in advance, and I do not anticipate that the onlooker will share my viewpoint. However, I feel that if my photograph leaves an image on his mind, something has been accomplished.' - Robert Frank

'I'm always mentally photographing everything as practice.' - Minor White

'Sometimes photographers mistake emotion for what makes a great photograph.' - Garry Winogrand

'Friendship based solely upon gratitude is like a photograph; with time it fades.' - Carmen Sylva

ABOUT THE AUTHOR

Marcel Borgstijn (1971) is an amateur photographer from the Netherlands. He loves to go out in nature for landscape photography. Furthermore he is into portraiture and conceptual photography.

Want to get in touch?
You can try one of the following:

Web: www.borgstijn.nl
Email: borgstijn@gmail.com
Twitter: @marcelborgstijn
Facebook: www.facebook.com/marcelborgstijn.1

Blogging at www.unleash-creativity.com where posts with creative photos & projects help you to unleash your own creativity in photography.
Definitely worth a visit!

Unleash Creativity